Michael Synk

Helping Minds Converge
Memphis, Tennessee

Copyright © 2001 by Michael Synk

All rights reserved. No part of this book may be reproduced or transmitted in any form or by any means, electronic or mechanical, including photocopying, recording, or by any information storage and retrieval system, without permission in writing from the publisher.

The Cheers *Model of Marketing: How to Create Customers as Loyal as Norm Peterson* is available for $11.95. Multiple copies may be purchased by contacting the publisher:

IN-SYNK, HELPING MINDS CONVERGE
1599 Vinton Avenue
Memphis, TN 38104
Tel.: 901-276-0200
Fax: 425-962-5188
e-Mail: msynk@in-synk.com
www.in-synk.com

Publisher's Cataloging-in-Publication Data
Synk, Michael.
    How to create customers as loyal as Norm Peterson: the "Cheers"model of marketing /Michael Synk. -- Memphis, TN : In-Synk, 2001.
    p.   cm.
    SUMMARY: The principles of customer relationship management are memorably illustrated in the valuable relationship between Norm Peterson and "Cheers".
    ISBN 0-9708409-0-X

    1. Customer Services. 2. Consumer satisfaction. 3. Customer loyalty. I. Cheers (Television program) II. Cheers model of marketing III. Title.

HF5415.5 .S96	2001	2001-087002
658.812	dc—21	CIP

05 04 03 02 01 ↔ 5 4 3 2 1
Cover design by Jeff Joiner
Project Coordination by Jenkins Group, Inc. • www.bookpublishing.com

Printed in the United States of America

Contents

	Acknowledgments 5
Chapter 1	Everybody Knows His Name 9
Chapter 2	It Goes Way Beyond the Beer 12
Chapter 3	It's Not Just a Television Fantasy 14
Chapter 4	The Basics of CRM and the Cheers Model 19
Chapter 5	Determining Your "Norms" 26
Chapter 6	Calculating Strategic Value 31
Chapter 7	Different Types of Norms 36
Chapter 8	Going Beyond Types: The Hierarchy of Need................ 39
Chapter 9	Different Marketing Plans for Each Customer 46

Chapter 10 The Cheers Model Is Everyone's
          Responsibility..................... 49

Chapter 11 The Birth of the Cheers Model of
          Marketing 53

Chapter 12 The Cheers Model at Work:
          A Case Study 57

Chapter 13 Why the Cheers Model? 61

          About the Author.................. 63

Acknowledgments

WHILE ACKNOWLEDGING everyone who made this book possible is just about impossible, there are a few people who deserve special recognition.

Ron Edmonds, whose trip to his favorite restaurant in Manhattan while playing hooky from a seminar on CRM in Stamford, Connecticut, provided the inspiration for the theme of *The* Cheers *Model of Marketing*.

Dave Talley and the staff of Southern Eye Associates, who humored me when I tested the *Cheers* Model with them and subsequently demonstrated its effectiveness with a 50 percent increase in business in just one year without increased advertising or other marketing efforts.

Mike Lemm, who designed my logo. Our skull sessions together during the design process helped me define In-Synk.

Roger and Suzie Cotton, who cheerfully helped with production of the book, audiotapes, and videos, at substandard wages and with often obtuse direction from me. I think we are still friends.

And

Meg Synk, my editor and partner in life. She has edited much more in my life than this book, and each edit has been for the better. God, how I love her!

Chapter 1
Everyone Knows His Name

I<small>T HAPPENS EVERY TIME.</small> He steps into the bar and everyone calls out his name in unison to greet him. As he walks across the room, the staff arranges his stool at the end of the bar just the way he likes it. In the meantime, a bartender slips him a straight line, allowing him to rattle off one of the witty one-liners stored in the recesses of his mind. While he is distracted, the same bartender fills a glass with his favorite brand of beer, making sure it has just the right amount of head, and slides it down the bar so that it arrives at his seat at exactly the same time he does. He sits down, his friends gather round, and an evening of revelry begins.

If you were Norm Peterson and this happened to you every time you stepped into Cheers, would you ever consider going anywhere else to drink beer? Isn't this the type of relationship you would like to have with each one of your best customers? Wouldn't you like them coming back again and again and again, just like Norm?

Norm Peterson might be a fictional character from a feel-good TV show about everybody's favorite bar, but his relationship with Cheers is worth examining. Under close scrutiny, it depicts a level of customer loyalty rarely achieved in the real world. It provides a meaningful metaphor for understanding and unleashing the concepts of Customer Relationship Management (CRM). Cheers has a relationship with Norm that goes way beyond the transaction of ordering a beer. Think about what everyone knows about Norm. It goes way beyond his name. They know how much beer he drinks. They know his tastes and preferences. They know his job history and family history. They know his friends and enemies. They know when he comes and goes. They know what he wants before he asks for it. In short, they know everything there is to know about him.

More importantly, they act on it. Cheers has managed to customize the delivery of a rather mundane product around Norm's exact needs. He gets what he wants, the way he wants it, without asking for it. Cheers has a relationship with Norm that has been nurtured and nursed over time, so that his needs can be anticipated. They have a learning relationship that continues to grow, all of it based on the principles of Customer Relationship Marketing expressed so eloquently in the words of the *Cheers* theme.

The Cheers Theme (Where Every Knows Your Name)*
    Sometimes you want to go
    Where everybody knows your name,
    And they're always glad you came;
    You wanna be where you can see,
    Our troubles are all the same;
    You wanna be where everybody knows your name.
    You wanna go where people know,
    People are all the same;
    You wanna go where everybody knows your name.

They know his name and his needs and Norm keeps coming back for more.

*The Cheers Theme (Where Everybody Knows Your Name), by Gary Portnoy and Judy Hart Angelo

Chapter 2
It Goes Way Beyond the Beer

THE AMAZING THING about Norm's relationship with Cheers is that it isn't about the beer at all. It goes way beyond the beer. The same is true about your loyal customers.

Think about all of Norm's options for enjoying a beer. There must be hundreds of them in Boston: bars, restaurants, liquor stores. If Norm were solely interested in the quality of the beer, any establishment that sold his favorite brand would do. It isn't about the price of beer either. If that were the case, he would pick up a case or two of his favorite brew at the liquor store and enjoy it in the familiar environs of his home. It isn't even about the atmosphere at Cheers, albeit a good one. Other taverns in Boston have his brand, at the right price, with good people gathered around.

So why does Norm come back to Cheers time and time again? Norm and all the other loyal customers of Cheers come back because Sam Malone and his staff address other needs of their customers, ones not related to beer. Sam identifies the customers who have the most potential value to Cheers, and for each one determines what he can do to keep them coming back. In delivering the beer, he finds ways to deliver that something extra that helps the customer with his or her higher needs.

The result is that each valuable customer of Cheers gets his or her beer the way he or she wants it, delivered in a way that is truly unique. Norm gets special service that meets his specific needs. The same is true for Cliff, Frasier, Paul and all the other valuable customers of Cheers.

Even though they all get the same product, they each receive it in a truly special way. Is it any surprise they never consider going elsewhere?

Chapter 3
It's Not Just a TV Fantasy

THIS SPECIALIZED service is not just a fantasy on TV. More and more companies are rejecting the traditional one-size-fits-all approach in favor of Customer Relationship Management methods. amazon.com, Saturn, and the Four Seasons Hotel, to name just a few that I have had the pleasure of learning about, have chosen to create long-term loyal relationships with their customers by giving each one just what he or she needs.

amazon.com keeps a detailed history of every book, tape, toy and gizmo a customer orders. When I log onto their site, they greet me with a list of books they recommend for me based on what I have ordered from them in the past. Occasionally I take them up on one of their suggestions and buy something from the list. The experience never fails to provide delight. I go back again and again not just because the price is right, or the convenience is superb. In fact, I have other options such as Barnes and Noble or Borders that in some ways can provide superior service. I go to back to amazon.com because of the learning relationship they have with me. They know what I have needed in the past and they anticipate my needs before I am even aware of them. Why wouldn't I go back?

I have had the same kind of experiences with my local Saturn dealership. A few years ago I bought a used Saturn sedan. When I took it in the first time, they checked the vehicle identification number and entered it into their database. They immediately realized I was the new owner of the car. After checking the database for the service history of my car, they told me the car was not yet due for the tune-up and transmission inspection I had come in for, but fixed what it really needed, saving me a substantial sum of money.

This type of behavior at a car dealership was foreign

to me. Service departments typically talk you into getting more service, not less. My faith in them grew so that when I received the periodic postcard telling me it was time for an oil change, I happily drove the thirty minutes to Saturn rather than to the Jiffy Lube around the corner. You can be sure that the next time I purchase a car, the first dealership I visit will be my friends at Saturn.

My friend David Talley has had a similar experience with Four Seasons Hotels chain. Dave is an optometrist and lecturer on the diagnoses and treatment of eye disease. When an optometric society in New England invited him to come and speak to their group, he was fortunate enough to be put up at the Four Seasons Hotel in Boston. After his lecture he went back to his room to wind down with a quiet meal from room service. Even though they weren't on the menu, Dave asked if it might be possible to get some oatmeal chocolate chip cookies. Being the fine establishment that it is, the hotel sent someone out and returned with the desired cookies.

That's a pretty good story, and at the rates you pay at a place like the Four Seasons, they *ought* to run out in the middle of the night to get you whatever you want. But it gets better. About six months later, Dave was invited to lecture in Chicago and, as luck would have it, he stayed in the local Four Seasons Hotel. After the lecture Dave went back to his room to relax with a late-night meal. He called to place his order and was greeted with, "Dr. Talley, I'm glad you called, would you like some of those oatmeal chocolate chip cookies you had the last time you stayed with us?" As you can imagine, Dave stays at a Four Seasons Hotel whenever he has an opportunity.

Even relationship-challenged businesses like your local supermarket are trying to create loyalty with their customers though CRM techniques. At many of them you can get a small swipe card that entitles the bearer to special discounts. As you go through checkout, you swipe the card into a little electronic scanner and your discounts are subtracted from your bill. The swipe card enables the store to track your purchase amounts and brand preferences, creating a history. From this history they send you coupons and discounts tailored to your specific needs. They even extend coupons for items related to your commonly purchased items. Your neighbors who purchase the same amount of groceries you do, receive entirely different coupons and discounts based on their different needs and preferences. The one-size-fits-all mentality is slowly dying even at the supermarket.

But you don't need these examples to convince you of the viability of the *Cheers* model. Each of you has places where you shop or vendors you order from who are your first and exclusive choices. The thought of changing them is abhorrent. It would be too much trouble. They serve almost too well. If you examine your relationship with them, you will find that this is because you have Norm-like experiences, similar to the ones described above.

The *Cheers* Model of Marketing isn't about Norm or beer or Sam's delivery of beer. It's about learning the principles of CRM through the eyes of Norm and Sam and then applying them at your company. This book will guide you through the process of first learning and then implementing The *Cheers* Model of Marketing so that you, too, will enjoy the benefits of having customers as loyal as Norm.

Chapter 4
The Basics of CRM and the Cheers Model

BEFORE YOU CAN implement the *Cheers* Model of Marketing, we need to examine a few key principles of CRM, as they will impact every facet of your business. They tend to go against the grain of traditional business wisdom that has been taught for the past fifty years. Ironically, they are so are rooted in common sense that the insight they provide can easily be overlooked the way one overlooks the wisdom of an old cliché. Acceptance of these principles will have a profound impact on your strategic and operational thinking.

Traditional wisdom says to focus on building market share through mass marketing appeals. At Cheers, if Sam Malone were interested in building market share, he would try to attract as many people to the bar as possible. To do that he might host a ladies night or a half price night, or maybe even hire a popular band that would bring in more customers. Each of these strategies is, for lack of a better name, a cattle call. The idea is to get as many new customers as possible. Whether those customers come back another time is highly dependent on whether the same special is offered again. Income or increased business is dependent to a large degree on tactics and not on relationships with customers. While this is a legitimate strategy, it is not the one Sam employs.

Sam and other practitioners of the *Cheers* Model of Marketing are more concerned with building the share of the business they have with each of their customers. Sam focuses on the size of Norm's entire beer budget, not just what he drinks at Cheers, and then finds ways to make it easier for Norm to spend more of that budget with him. He wants Norm to come back again and again. It's called building your share of customer. Sam Malone is building his share of Norm's beer tab; Saturn, its share of my driveway; amazon.com, its share of my bookshelf; Four Seasons Hotel, its share of Dave Talley's hotel nights; your supermarket, its share of your grocery basket.

Likewise, any practitioner of CRM or the *Cheers* Model of Marketing is focused on building their share of customer. Creating a clever "share of" is a perfect way of focusing on your company's marketing direction.

If you adopt a "share of customer" outlook rather than a market share outlook, the next change in principle is to focus on the strategic value of each customer rather than their actual value. Strategic value provides a better way of prioritizing the efforts put into building relationships.

Actual value is easy and exact to calculate—you just have to tally up the fees or charges the customer has paid you. Strategic value is the total value a customer could deliver to a company and the company's strategic partners if it delivered all of its business to them. It's an estimate, not an exact figure like actual value. But when compared to actual value, it provides a focus that actual value alone cannot produce.

Imagine the motivation created when a customer's strategic value is determined to be twice, thrice, or four times that of actual value. The need to get to know the customer's long-term needs becomes essential to building the share of customer.

Norm's strategic value includes the value of the beer in his refrigerator, the beer he consumes at other drinking establishments, and the additional beer drunk by those enjoying his company in the bar. For amazon.com, my strategic value includes not just the books I buy but the other product lines they offer such as tapes, electronics and toys.

At Saturn, strategic value goes beyond the two cars in my driveway and charges for maintenance and repairs—it extends to future cars I might buy for my children, business, and cars bought by people I recommend the dealership to.

The Four Seasons Hotels estimate Dave Talley's value to include his business travel, vacation travel, business and social meals, meetings, banquets, gift shop items, etc., in every city he visits that has a Four Seasons. It includes the value going to strategic partners such as airlines, caterers, florists, spas, and restaurants.

At your supermarket, strategic value extends past groceries and on to other items such as banking, pharmacy and catering needs. In any case, strategic value has the power to magnify the importance of retaining valuable customers and expanding the relationship with them.

The third and fourth principles seem almost too obvious to state. Every customer has different tastes and preferences, and different customers should be treated differently. Somehow these simple truths have become clear as mud. Whether the cause is production efficiency, accounting simplicity or mass marketing methods, a preponderance of one-size-fits-all rules of engagement keeps companies from building personal relationships with their customers.

True practitioners of CRM acknowledge that customers have different needs and therefore require different rules of engagement. They create production, accounting, and marketing support systems that support these third and fourth principles.

At Cheers, while virtually everyone comes to get the same thing, a drink, each customer has different reasons for coming and different ways they want the drink served, and in each case different needs are satisfied.

Although Saturn has a limited product line and even a non-negotiating pricing strategy, they don't try to sell their cars to everybody, only to people whose needs the auto fits, and they are only too happy to customize delivery and service to meet your specific needs.

The people of amazon.com have each customer's reading and listening habits individually identified so that they can recommend additional purchases.

Dave Talley's profile with Four Seasons Hotels reflects his preferences, not those of the guest in the room next to his. His room is set up with the magazines he reads and, as we have already found out, his room service options include oatmeal chocolate chip cookies. The guest in the next room has different magazines and a different room service menu.

Even supermarkets are stocking their shelves with your specific needs in mind.

Build your share of customer, focus on strategic value, acknowledge that every customer has different tastes and preferences, and treat different customers differently. These words should become your mantra and the mantra of your co-workers if you are to successfully implement the *Cheers* Model of Marketing. But a mantra alone won't make it happen. The *Cheers* Model of Marketing involves more than what meets the eye and impacts more than the sales and service departments of your company. It means the entire organization understands and then acts with the basic principles of CRM at the forefront of their minds. The remaining chapters deal with the specific tasks that need to be completed to make the *Cheers* model a reality.

Chapter 5
Determining Your "Norms"

THE FIRST STEP in implementing the *Cheers* model is analyzing your customer base. You need to identify your best customers—your "Norms"—and take at closer look at the rest of the list. If done in an objective and thorough manner, you'll find "Norms" that you never knew you had, you'll identify potential 'Norms" to take to the next level, and you will isolate those customers that will never be "Norms" for you.

This important first step sets priorities for your whole organization. It focuses your efforts on your best customers and keeps you from being distracted by trying to bend over backwards for every customer that calls.

We start by doing an 80/20 analysis of your customer base. The famous 80/20 rule touted by many consultants contends that 80 percent of any company's revenue is obtained from 20 percent of their customers. Sam Malone can't afford to reserve a stool at the bar for everyone who walks into *Cheers*, but he can give that level of service to the 20 percent who keep the bills paid.

Create a spreadsheet that lists all your customers from the last twelve months. In the first column put the customer; in the second column, the corresponding dollar amount they were invoiced in the last twelve months. Sort the customers from highest to lowest value. When this is completed, add up the total revenue of all these customers, and calculate 80% of that number. Then, start at the top of the list, with your highest revenue-producing customers and add up their totals until you reach the 80 percent figure. How many of your customers are responsible for 80 percent of your sales revenue? Figure the percentage of the total number of customers that this 80 percent revenue group represents. If the number is much higher than 20 percent I would be quite surprised.

Most of your Norms appear on this "A" list that makes up 80 percent of your business. But some of your Norms probably aren't there, and some of the customers on that list aren't really Norms. The analysis done thus far only takes into account the dollar value of the customer.

Now we need to look at the effort expended to serve each customer.

Follow the same instructions above, but instead of entering revenue figures into the second column, enter a transactional figure such as number of invoices, or number of orders placed. This transactional 80/20 analysis should give you a better handle on who your Norms really are. Compare your list of highest value customers to your list of highest transactional customers. They are not the same, are they? Which list of customers are you more familiar with? Most companies are more familiar with the transactional list; they place more orders so their names come up more often. You are probably surprised by some of the names on the lists. Some of your most familiar customers will not be on that revenue list, and some of your best customers will have slipped onto the list unnoticed because their number of transactions is low. With the *Cheers* model you will be very aware of your sources of revenue and everyone in the company will be able to rattle off your top ten customers.

At this point start trying to make sense of what is on your various lists. Rank all of your customers according to what you have learned about their real value and your intuitions about their potential. The ones at the top of your list are most likely your Norms. These are the customers you are already doing a good job of serving. Your goal is to find ways to make them so loyal that they wouldn't dream of using someone else. Now tailor your operating methods and practices around their needs so that doing business with you is the most rewarding part of their day.

Now look at the rest of the customers on your list. The bulk of these, your "B" list, probably have many of the same characteristics of your Norms, but are not currently as valuable. They are in the same line of business, or are of similar size, or use similar technologies, but they just haven't used your product or services as much. Your goal is to concentrate on building your share of customer with these potential Norms. Because they already know you and you are already set up to deal with customers like them (your Norms), you are more than halfway there.

Now let's look at that group down at the bottom of the revenue list. These customers will probably never be Norms. Their value is low and their transactions numerous. You could build up business with them, one at a time, but they probably have requirements much different from the rest of your business. While you are struggling to shape your existing structure around their needs, you endanger your relationship with your Norms. Some you are happy to work with, so perhaps you can set up an alternative channel for them that minimizes your efforts and distractions. Think about Lilith at Cheers. Sure she gets a stool at the bar, but only because six people get up and leave when they see her walk in. Maybe you should let your competitors serve the Liliths.

Chapter 6
Calculating Strategic Value

Now that you have figured out who your Norms and potential Norms are, your next task is to estimate the strategic value of each one. In the previous exercise you used actual value to rank your customers. But actual value alone limits your ability to focus on building the share of customer that the *Cheers* model is founded on. To emphasize the difference, let's examine the difference between Norm's actual value to Cheers and his strategic value.

A formula that reflects Norm's actual value would

include three elements: price, quantity and time period. It could be written in any number of ways, but would likely be something like this:

(Price of Beer x Beers Per Week) x Number of Weeks = Norm's Actual Value

or

(PB x BPW) x NW = NAV

As you can see, this isn't rocket science. But it is a useful tool for quickly sizing up a customer's value. Based on a week or two's observation, a bartender can make a pretty accurate guess about a new customer's value. Let's plug in some numbers. Let's assume the price of beer is $2.00 and Norm drinks forty beers a week and comes to the bar virtually every day of the week for a year. The formula looks like this:

($2.00 x 40) x 52 = $4,160.00

This simple formula could be applied to every customer that comes through the door. I recommend you write an actual value formula for your business, similar to the one used above. Include all the elements: prices, quantity and time period. Adjust the formula to match the cycles and structure of your business and keep it simple. Then insist on its use.

But using it alone isn't good enough. An actual value formula doesn't take into account the potential value of a customer to a company and/or the company's strategic partners. What we need is a strategic value formula for Norm. We start with the actual value formula we wrote earlier, but we add three or more other elements depending on the business. The first element is products or services purchased or consumed elsewhere, or "competitive" value. The second element is "influential" value, the value of other customers that will be influenced by the customer. I call the third element "developmental" value, the potential income derived by creating complementary products and services or delivering them though partnerships with other companies. When we add these elements to the actual value formula it looks like this:

(PB x BPW) x NW + <u>B</u>eers <u>D</u>runk <u>E</u>lsewhere + <u>B</u>eers <u>D</u>runk <u>N</u>ear <u>N</u>orm + <u>B</u>ar <u>F</u>ood <u>B</u>eyond <u>P</u>retzels = <u>N</u>orm's <u>S</u>trategic <u>V</u>alue

or

(PB x BPW) x NW + BDE + BDNN + BFBP = NSV

Again, this isn't an exact science, but it is an effective tool for determining how much more value there is within a customer. Let's make some assumptions and plug in some new numbers to see what Norm's strategic value is. I think we can reasonably assume that Norm has a few six-packs a week at home (BDE = $10.00 x 52 weeks). Everyone drinks more beer than usual when Norm is there, possibly equal to what Norm drinks collectively (BDNN = Norm's actual value). And what if Cheers could feed Norm by working out a partnership with the restaurant upstairs or by opening a kitchen to prepare sandwiches ($6.00 a day x five days a week x fifty-two weeks a year = BFBP). The formula looks like this:

$$[(\$2.00 \times 40) \times 52] + \$520.00 + \$4{,}160.00 + \$1{,}560.00 = \$10{,}400.00$$

Using strategic value instead of actual value, Norm's importance to Cheers more than doubles. The staff of Cheers can instantly recognize that Norm's value extends beyond himself to other patrons. The simple strategy of selling six packs from a cooler in the back could be employed to build share of customer. A more complex strategy of making lunch available would increase share of customer not only for Norm but for others as well.

In other industries, a customer's potential can triple, quadruple or even more. Imagine the change in focus within your company if strategic value is used to create and implement sales and retention strategies. Besides emphasizing new opportunities for growth, the downside of losing a customer is more apparent as well. At the same time you create many ideas for expanding your product line. Test this out by creating a Strategic Value Formula for your customers that matches your industry and company. Recalculate the value of all the Norms and Norm-wannabes that you ranked in the previous chapter. You'll find that you will be thinking differently about your customers. Your focus will become sharpened. The importance of each customer will become heightened.

Chapter 7
Different Types of Norms

Now that you have determined your Norms and potential Norms and have calculated the strategic value of each, the next step is figure out what and how many types of Norms you have. There is an old adage that makes sense here: "Birds of a feather flock together." For the purposes of the *Cheers* Model of Marketing, you can translate that cliché to mean that similar types of customers will use your product or service in similar ways.

Typing works this way: Suppose you have a product

that works well in the financial industry. If Bank A uses your product in a unique way, it is highly likely that Bank B would want to use your product in a similar way when you tell them about it. As you work with Bank A to customize your product for their needs, you will learn things about their business that will help you to anticipate Bank B's needs. What succeeds with one will likely succeed for others of the same type.

Examine your Norms and potential Norms. Sort them by industry type, size, technologies used, geography, or type of customer they serve. Use names that make sense to you; sophistication is not necessary. If your customers are all in the same industry, figure out the distinctions between them and sort along those distinctions.

The benefits of typing like this are enormous. First, you will increase profits by grouping like customers and streamlining procedures to work with them more efficiently. Then, you'll be able to expand business by selling the good things you are doing with your best customers to new ones of similar type. You can offer "B" list customers the same "customization" you put into place for your Norms in the same industry. Because the groundwork has already been laid, there will be no need to radically change service and delivery methods.

Typing is an instant roadmap for sales strategies that deliver faster growth. And the best part is that you won't be losing your best customers because your attention is diverted to one who might never be a Norm of yours.

Chapter 8

Going Beyond Types: The Hierarchy of Need

THE EFFORT TO achieve your ultimate goal of treating every customer differently cannot stop at typing. Although typing identifies similarities between customers, it doesn't mean similar customers are the same. The hierarchy of need refers to customers' basic needs, their delivery needs and their higher needs. When you understand and act upon the hierarchy of need of each customer, you will capture their loyalty.

Norm's basic need is beer. If you can serve him a beer the cash register will ring. A good rule of thumb for determining the basic need of your customers is related to that sound. Ask yourself what makes the cash register ring within your organization. What is it that your customer will pay for that you can provide? For Cheers the basic product or service is beer, which matches up nicely with Norm's basic need.

There are plenty of other establishments that can deliver beer as well as Cheers can, many of them at lower prices. This is true of your business also. No matter the product or service, someone else can make it or deliver it or serve it up as well you can (or maybe even better than you can). Even if you have a monopoly or technological advantage, eventually someone will come along to challenge you by making or delivering your product as well or better than you do.

If Cheers relied only on having Norm's brand at the price he wanted, it would eventually be giving it to him, not a profitable endeavor for any business. If you rely solely on that same strategy you, too, will eventually be giving it away. The fact of the matter is that a competitor eventually will come up with the same or better product at the same or better price.

Remember when Norm was wooed away from Cheers by what appeared to be the perfect job, taste tester at a brewery? The only thing better than the beer at Cheers was free beer, or so it seemed to Norm. But after a brief period of bliss, he came to hate his new job and even to despise beer. He realized that there was more being delivered at Cheers than beer. Sam and the crew addressed the more important needs of his life and were soon missed.

Cheers doesn't rely solely on serving Norm's basic need. They have identified his delivery needs. Delivery needs can be defined as the needs of the customer related to the basic need that make it easier and more enjoyable for him to buy the product. Norm's delivery needs center around three things. The first is his need for routine. Norm wants his brand, he wants it in a certain glass, with a certain amount of head, at the same stool, with the same friends gathered around, the same way every time. So Cheers' delivery of the beer follows that routine.

Norm's second delivery need is related to his cash flow problems. He is regularly short on cash. Cheers runs a tab for him to make it easier for him to purchase beer.

His third need is enjoyment. Norm likes to have a good time when he drinks his beer. He likes to tell jokes and has an encyclopedic list of one-liners to share. Someone behind the bar makes it his business to feed him a straight line when he enters the bar and regularly thereafter.

You can address the delivery needs of your customers too. Ask yourself what procedures or methods you can put in place that make it easier and more enjoyable for them to buy from you. How can you more easily take their orders? Can special procedures be implemented just for them? What about shipping and packaging to suit special requirements? Customized delivery is limited only by your creativity.

But as you have probably already surmised, it doesn't take long for competitors to figure out and then offer the same things. As they say, "Imitation is the sincerest form of flattery." Before long, your methods will be duplicated and extended to others, leaving you with the need to search for more and more customization.

Thankfully, Norm has higher needs that can be acted upon. Norm is a lonely guy. If Cheers can satisfy his need for camaraderie while delivering the beer, they have helped him out in life. In fact, the employees of Cheers have become close friends of his and they guard his friendship dearly. They make sure that only the right kind of people get the opportunity to make his acquaintance. They are also aware of Norm's need to play practical jokes. He is involved in every instance of tomfoolery in the bar; he is actually used to instigate various nefarious plans against unsuspecting patrons. They also know that Norm is quite the competitor and loves a good game. Whether it is bowling, basketball or Irish coffee contests, Norm is a part of the team that takes on the foes from Gary's Old Time Tavern. In all of these activities, Cheers is trying to satisfy Norm's higher needs in life. They are helping him with more important things than beer and, in so doing, are developing the loyalty that has him coming back every single day.

Now look at Cliff and Frazier. Do they get treated like Norm? No. Do they get treated as they like? Yes. Cliff gets a steady stream of unsuspecting victims he can regale with stories of mind-numbing disinformation. Frazier gets his ego boosted by surrounding himself with his "intellectual inferiors." They all get to be part of a close-knit community.

You develop loyalty with your customers by satisfying their needs at every level. When you address the higher needs of your customer while delivering your basic product well, you earn an allegiance that your competitors will find hard to duplicate. When you operate in a business-to-business setting you can work on two fronts: The larger business needs and your contacts' personal needs. What are the larger business problems your customer has? Can you in some way help them run their business better? Reduce expenses? Increase revenue?

Also address the personal needs of the customer. Such things as more time with the kids or extra rounds on the golf course are the things that matter here. The focus here is higher needs, no matter how unrelated to the basic product and its delivery.

But again, you must attend to all three parts of that hierarchy of need. Your company has to deliver the basic need at least as well if not better than the competition if the loyalty engendered by addressing the higher need is to continue. If Sam started cutting corners by watering down the beer, Norm would be gone in a heartbeat. And in the reverse situation, if you serve only the basic need, a potentially loyal relationship becomes a transaction. The customer focuses on the deal at hand and will soon seek out better ones. Rest assured that a better deal will come along.

As you get further and further into understanding your customers, you will see that even the same types of customers with the same basic and delivery needs have different higher needs, needs that reflect the intricacies of their businesses and personal lives. Each one of them deserves to be treated differently.

Chapter 9

Different Marketing Plans for Each Customer

THE CHEERS MODEL transforms our understanding of marketing plans. Now each individual customer has a marketing plan built around his or her unique needs. At Cheers, Norm has one plan, Cliff has another, Frasier has still another. A new plan is conceived and implemented with each new customer, because every customer is different and deserves to be treated that way.

It's a bottoms up strategy (no pun intended). If you asked Sam if he had a marketing plan for Cheers, he wouldn't know how to answer you. But if you asked him how he was building his business, he would tell you that he was doing it "one customer at a time." In fact, his overall marketing plan is really a compilation of the individual marketing plans he has for each of his customers. Everything else flows from his intimate knowledge of his customers: his advertising, his public relations efforts, and his new product and service offerings. With this model, customers can be counted on to return. Revenue grows steadily as relationships with new customers grow. Satisfaction is high. Building the business is steady, logical, and enjoyable.

Contrast this with conventional marketing plans. The standard approach goes something like this: A new product is developed. A plan is developed to market the product. It includes public relations, advertising, and sales strategies to create awareness of the product and a desire for it. The customer's needs are almost an afterthought.

It's a top down approach. It focuses on building market share rather than share of customer. Customers tend to be treated the same. The focus is on the product, not the customer. New customers come in the front door, but older ones sneak out the back door. Revenue grows quickly but erratically. Satisfaction fluctuates. Building the business also builds tension.

Believing in the *Cheers* model means writing individual marketing plans for each of your Norms and potential Norms. Start by charting out the hierarchy of needs for the customer. Calculate their actual and strategic values and post them on the chart. Consider what type the customer should be classified with and post that information, too. When the chart is completed, review the profile you just created and let your intuitions take over. Produce a list of actions to be taken that addresses all of the customer's needs: basic, delivery and higher. Prioritize the list and start working your way through it.

This list is your marketing plan. It impacts everything. Make your other marketing decisions, such as advertising and public relations, based on the compilation of the individual marketing plans. Write the plan down in pencil, because it won't be static. It's a work in progress that can change with each and every interaction. Be prepared to go with the flow to wherever the customer takes you.

Chapter 10

The Cheers *Model Is Everyone's Responsibility*

NOW THAT YOU understand the concept of the *Cheers* model, the challenging part will be getting everyone on the team involved in it. The *Cheers* Model of Marketing isn't the sole preserve of the sales team or marketing department or the customer service staff. It requires the participation of everyone who interacts with customers, which means everyone in your organization.

The sales, marketing, and service people might "own" the relationship because they have more "face" or "ear" time with a customer, but each individual plays a part in understanding the hierarchy of need and the building of marketing plans. Information about your customers drips into your organization in a multitude of places. Accounting collects information about payment terms and schedules. The warehouse learns about delivery opportunities. Engineering learns about the manufacturing process. Tech support flags down problems they have with your product. The list of collection points is limited only by the size of your organization.

The fact is that your customers are talking to you regularly, giving hints about their needs. Unfortunately, in too many companies, employees don't pick up on such hints. Maybe they are unaware of the importance of the information that reaches their desks. Possibly they don't know what to look for or don't realize that what they learn needs to be shared. Maybe they mistakenly believe that relationship building is the job of sales or marketing or customer service rather than being a part of their duties, too.

To overcome this obstacle and to make full use of the *Cheers* Model of Marketing, the organization has to doggedly pursue a practice of complete information sharing. Information, wherever collected, must quickly and efficiently be passed to whomever in the organization is best positioned to act on it. It also has to be compiled in some sort of a repository so that it can be used in building the marketing plan.

Likewise, the marketing plan must be shared with everyone else so that they will know how to recognize a drip of information when it drops on their desk. Finally, when information is acted upon in such a way as to improve the relationship and increase business, the success story must be passed on back to the collections source. This reinforces the acts of collecting and sharing and ensures that they become habits rather than passing fads.

The folks at Cheers are especially good at sharing information. It all starts with Sam. He's the focal point of the information flow. The other bartenders and the waitresses collect information about customers and feed him what they find out. Sam processes the information and matches it up with the profile he has in his head of each customer. Then he feeds back to the waitress or bartender what they need to know to move the relationship forward. He lives by the saying, "Nothing shared, nothing gained."

The free flow of information at Cheers can be duplicated at your company. Of course Cheers has it easier. They are in a bar. They can shout out the info. Staff meetings are merely a matter of having a huddle behind the bar. But with a little ingenuity and some technology, you can do it, too. Sam's head is the marketing database where the collected information is stored and later dispersed. The waitresses and bartenders are the various departments that collect the information and interact with the customer.

You will notice that the role of marketing director changes in the *Cheers* model. The focus is now customer retention instead of conversion. An additional and maybe even more important role is that of information manager. The marketing manager is responsible for making sure everyone in the organization has the information readily available to them to build better relationships with the customers.

As you move to implement the *Cheers* Model of Marketing, spend a lot of time figuring out how to keep the information flow going. If it ever stops, the *Cheers* model will also stop.

Chapter 11

The Birth of the Cheers Model of Marketing

THE CHEERS MODEL of Marketing was born in December of 1998. For several months I had been struggling with the task of teaching customer relationship management to the ophthalmology practices owned by my employer. Although CRM was a perfect fit for the referral-based practices we operated, each business example I used to illustrate the relevance of CRM was rejected out of hand. "We're not in that business; we're doctors." "Those examples don't apply to us; medicine is different."

While I was willing to concede that eye care was more complex than most businesses, I was adamant that a CRM approach would make our referring doctors more loyal, and they would then send more patients our way. I was convinced that we would enjoy a substantial increase in revenue without enduring a corresponding increase in advertising and marketing expenses. But how could I convince the skeptics in the practices?

During a break in the workday, a co-worker was discussing his recent dinner at his favorite restaurant in New York City. He hadn't been there in several years, but while attending a CRM workshop in nearby Stamford, Connecticut, he skipped out on a session and made his way to the city and this restaurant. Witnesses confirmed that when he walked in the door, the bartender immediately greeted him by name, poured his favorite scotch without asking and inquired about his long absence. After a round of drinks, he and his friends were whisked away to a table where the pampering continued. Everyone knew his name and what he wanted, all without asking. I said to myself, "No wonder he goes back whenever he's within a hundred miles. This is a real-life example of that Norm-guy on the *Cheers* TV show. How can we create that same relationship with our referring doctors?"

Within a week of that conversation, the director of our local practice stopped by to tell me he was ready to try the CRM approach. Could I teach his entire staff how it works? He would give me a half-hour at his next six staff meetings to present the concept. What a break! I accepted the challenge on the condition that he accept some unusual training methods.

He was in a tough spot. The center historically had less-than-ideal relationships with its referring doctors. Although the quality of care was as good or better than any practice in the area, the referrals were reluctant ones at best. Competitive practices were strong and growing and definitely courting our constituents. Our service was good but not good enough to inspire loyalty.

The staff wasn't motivated to improve things, either. Staff members perceived their responsibilities narrowly. Even though each staff member interacted with referring doctors and their patients, no one felt accountable for building relationships with them. Each person's tunnel vision kept him or her from seeing the impact they could have on increasing business from the referring doctors.

It was in this setting, armed with my knowledge and convictions about CRM, that I unleashed my secret weapon: Norm Peterson and the *Cheers* Model of Marketing. At the first meeting, I presented the relationship between Norm and Cheers as the model relationship between a business and its customer (Chapter One: Everyone Knows His Name). The response was overwhelming. Everyone could give me personal examples of relationships they had that were similar to the Norm/Cheers relationship. The Norm/Cheers relationship captured the imagination of the entire staff. I posed the question, "Wouldn't it be great to have the same relationship with our customers, the referring doctors? If, in the next five staff meetings, we discovered why Norm always comes back and it made sense, would you agree to apply what we learned to our referring doctors so that they will always refer their patients to us?" They did, and away we went.

Chapter 12

The Cheers Model at Work: A Case Study

THAT FIRST MEETING imprinted upon the staff the picture of the ideal relationship they wanted to have with their referring doctors. The remaining meetings dealt with making the ideal a reality. Using the Norm/Cheers analogy every step of the way, we explored the principles of CRM and applied them to complexities of the practice.

First we went through the process of determining which of their doctors were Norms, which were potential Norms, and which would probably never be Norms (Chapter Five, Determining Your "Norms"). We created an "ABCD" code that everyone used to identify and remember the loyalty and value of each doctor. Next we wrote strategic value formulas for the doctors (Chapter Six, Calculating Strategic Value). This helped us understand our share of customer with each doctor or "share of referrals" as we called it. Simple tracking methods were put in place to determine if we were gaining or losing share each with each doctor in each quarter.

With these measurements in place, we moved to the more qualitative aspects of CRM. We looked at all the different referring doctors, mostly optometrists, and created types that each could be fit into (Chapter Seven: Different Types of Norms). The staff determined that there were five types of optometrists: independent, large group, corporate franchised, corporate employed and academic. Non-optometric sources of referrals were a sixth type. Comparing the six categories, the staff could understand the similar needs of doctors of similar types.

A cross-functional team then created a database that detailed the hierarchy of needs for each doctor. They used a contact management software package, although it could have just as easily been done with paper. The fields were customized for easy input of the information that the staff felt was helpful in tracking the higher needs, such things as family status, certification requirements, education, hobbies, income needs, expenses, patient flow, etc. Finally, the director and marketing assistant created short five-step marketing plans for each doctor (Chapter Nine: Different Marketing Plans for Each Customer). Every quarter, each marketing plan would be evaluated and adjusted with an eye toward doing whatever possible to meet the higher needs of the doctor.

Finally, the staff recognized that all this work was for naught unless everyone participated (Chapter 10: The *Cheers* Model is Everyone's Responsibility). We developed a small contest to reinforce the habit of sharing information. For the first bit of information passed on that filled a database field on a doctor, a staff member would receive a candy bar. Five bits of useful information earned a coupon for a free video rental. An additional paid day of vacation came with twenty bits. Needless to say, the database filled up quickly, and we realized we knew more than we thought we did. The doctors were telling us all kinds of helpful things, and now we had them written down and could act on them. The marketing assistant prepared a weekly cheat sheet for all the staff. It listed the doctors they were most likely to interact with in the coming week based on the patients referred and scheduled. It included the doctor's "ABCD" designation, type, share of referrals, current step in the marketing plan and some up-to-date information with which to make small talk. The sheet also included success stories detailing information shared that had resulted in progress with the doctor's marketing plan. Both the contest and the cheat sheet provided just the right reinforcements to make information sharing a perpetual process.

The results spoke loudly. While the number of referring doctors rose only slightly, their referrals skyrocketed. Revenue increased almost 50 percent from the previous year while marketing expenses remained the same. The *Cheers* Model of Marketing made a dramatic difference in profitability.

Chapter 13

Why the Cheers Model?

THE *CHEERS* MODEL of Marketing is really just common sense that has become uncommon over the years. Think about how many experiences you have had with companies that have done a poor job of serving you or getting you to come back. Many places of business get your return business by default. They concentrate on short-term gain, moving the most product, getting you to buy what they have rather than what you want. Wouldn't it be nice if the reverse were more common? It is with the *Cheers* Model of Marketing.

But a more important case for the *Cheers* model exists. It's the case for survival. The *Cheers* Model of Marketing provides a means to retain your customers and create profitable new ones with less risk and more rewards. It's a vehicle for fending off your competitors and extending your security. It's a way to take care of your business while you take care of your customers. If you don't, you take the chance of losing your business. Norm explains it better in this interchange with Sam.

Sam: Hey! What's happening, Norm?

Norm: It's a dog eat dog world, Sammy, and I'm wearing milkbone underwear!

About the Author

Michael Synk is the President of In-Synk: Helping Minds Converge, an enterprise dedicated to helping business owners and executives get their teams and processes focused on the goals of their customers With over twenty years of successful business experience, Michael's approach to the essentials of organizational performance is insightful, motivational, and most important, practical.

Michael is working on his second book, *Lions That Roared!*, the story of the 1980 Holy Redeemer High School Track Team, a group of outcasts who taught their coach the basics of leadership and achievement. Michael lives in Memphis, Tennessee, with his wife Meg and three children. Golf is one of Michael's major motivations in life.